30 Days of Discipline

Practical Habits to Build Discipline and Focus in the Next 30 Days

By:
Raza Imam

Warning: This is <u>NOT</u> Theory

Are you **struggling** to stay **motivated**, **focused**, and **productive**?

Maybe you want to write a book, or get in shape, or start a business, or transform your relationship.

But every time you try you feel a ***growing*** sense of frustration that you haven't made progress. You know that you have big goals but can't stay focused and productive enough to make them happen.

Trust me, it's *more common* than you think.

The reality is that the longer you wait, the *worse* it gets.

But here's my warning to you:

You probably already know what you should be doing.

You ***don't*** need a special technique.

You ***don't*** need new research.

You ***don't*** need to do anything fancy.

You need to take action.

So if you want fluff, new techniques, theory, ground-breaking research, then please click off.

But if you want to instantly feel motivated, focused, and productive - keep reading.

And take action.

Because the good news is that it's **not** that difficult to do.

You'll discover how to go from frustrated to focused, *in just 60 seconds*, so
you feel and perform like a <u>CHAMPION</u>.

Message Me

This book is just the beginning.
Reach out to connect.
And take action.

Do you want help?

Do you want to go deeper?

Do you want to ask questions?

Do you want to see how to apply this in real life?

If this book sparks something in you, don't let it fade.

Connect with me here: linktr.ee/razaimam

📅 Book a 1:1 call

📞 Speak with me directly

📩 Join my private email list

🎁 Claim your free bonuses

🎥 See behind-the-scenes strategies

📱 DM me on LinkedIn, X, or Instagram

Reach out and take action.

All in one place: linktr.ee/razaimam
www.AuthorPreneurElite.com

Table of Contents

Short and Sweet – No Fluff

"Give me a one-page bullet-list of exactly what I should do. That's worth more to me than a stack of books that I have to dig through to get to the good stuff. I may give you 50 bucks for the books. But I'll pay you $5,000 for the one page."

That's a quote from Alwyn Cosgrove, a world-famous strength coach and entrepreneur.

In this short book, we've given you everything you need to know about staying focused and achieving your goals. This book is short, and that's for a reason.

We wanted to give you 100% actionable content, not a bunch of fluff and theory.

Sure we give practical examples to prove our point.

Yes, we give you specific action items to do and we explain why.

Of course we tell you exactly how to implement these steps to get the best results.

But we worked ***ruthlessly*** to keep this book short and sweet.

So remember to **take action!**

What Happened When I Got Focused and Disciplined

Like most 30-something guys with kids, I have a very busy life. Here's my typical day: An hour-long commute to and from work. Helping my 5 year-old with homework. Giving the kids baths. Putting them to bed. Doing dishes. Hanging out with the wife. And going to bed.

Not to mention the community service and volunteer work that I do, visiting friends and family on the weekends, and religious and spiritual commitments that I have.

Currently, I'm 34 with 3 kids, work a full-time job AND write books.

But it wasn't always like this for me.

For the longest time, I wanted to make a side income, in addition to my full-time job.

I tried everything; "creative" real estate, internet marketing, blogging, starting a consulting business, and multi-level marketing.

But nothing ever stuck.

After a while, I learned about search engine optimization and created a fitness blog. It started seeing some success so I decided to take my diet and workouts seriously.

It took a few years to finally figure out how to eat and the exact right workouts to do, but after I got the information down, **I started to focus.**

Well, within a few short months I got these results:

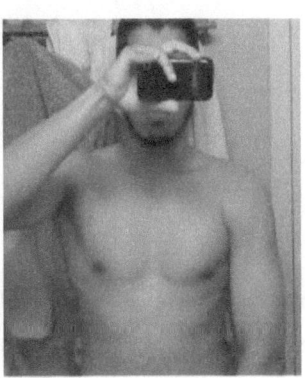 

So now that my fitness was where I wanted it to be, I decided to write a book.

I called it "***The Science of Getting Ripped***"

I **focused hard** on writing it, formatting it, publishing it and marketing it. After that, it became a bestseller in multiple categories.

Seeing these results was literally life-changing for me. I couldn't believe it.

It was all the result of me getting **focused and disciplined**.

And that's why I wrote this book.

My promise to you is that if you read this book, and follow the simple, detailed plan, you will be able to CRUSH your goals and turb0-charge your productivity as well.

Sincerely,
Raza Imam

Visualize Yourself Being Successful

One of the best self-help books of all time is Psycho-Cybernetics written by Dr. Maxwell Maltz in the 1960s. He was a plastic surgeon that noticed patients who have had their limbs amputated still felt pain in that limb.

Even though it had been amputated.

This got him thinking about self-image. He concluded that we become what we think about. He's not the first one to say this, but it really resonated with me.

The whole point of his book is that your mind is like a "heat-seeking missile." If it has a goal, infused with emotion and passion, it will figure out how to accomplish it.

There will be trial and error, but if you keep believing in your goal and take action, you will eventually achieve it. He gives the example of a baby reaching for an object on a table. When he first reaches for it, he might miss, but he will eventually get it.

So belief creates a positive self-image. When you create a positive self-image of yourself ALREADY having accomplished your goal, you will have the motivation and drive to figure it out.

Here's a brief meditation you can try:

Sit back, openly, confidently, and expectantly with your arms at your side and your head leaning back slightly.

Close your eyes and smile ever so slightly with your mouth and jaws loose and relaxed.

Imagine you're sitting on a cruise ship, looking out at a dark sky early in the morning. The horizon looks purple and is almost glowing. As you sit there, imagine a warm golden rain falling gently on your body.

Enjoy the beautiful peace, warmth, and serenity of this powerful scene.

Now imagine the goal that you seek to achieve. **Imagine yourself already having achieved it.**

Imagine the power, and confidence, and excitement, and enthusiasm, and gratitude you would feel once you're accomplished it.

KNOW in your mind that you've already achieved it.
That you already have it.
Feel those feelings.
Think those thoughts.

Know that this is the secret to achieving your goals is **to be thankful for already having achieved them.**

Feel it.

Believe it.

Expect it.

Doing this meditation for 5 minutes every day will mold your subconscious mind to expect that reality.

It will sharpen your focus, enhance your motivation, and help guide you to the actions and activities that you need to take to achieve them.

It's incredibly powerful.

Now go do it and enjoy the feelings of pride, confidence, gratitude, and excitement that come with it.

1). So choose a goal.

2). Imagine, visualize, and see yourself having already achieved it.

3). Sense the amazing feelings of achieving your goal.

4). Use the steps in this book to build focus so that you can create it in reality.

The Power of Focus

"The successful warrior is the average man,
with laser-like focus" – Bruce Lee

If you want to achieve anything in life, you need to know how to focus. You probably already know this. The reason why you're reading this book is that you also know that focus is hard to come by. Why? There are just so many things going on in our lives that compete for attention and focus. This is not rocket science. This is plainly obvious.

How often do you get derailed from your goals? How often do you wake up with a clear idea of what you'd like to accomplish for that day and go to bed having failed to accomplish your goals? Remember, it's not just you. This happens to the very best of us. It's just so easy to get caught up in our obligations, roles and activities that we don't have much focus left for the things that truly matter.

All of us have big goals. All of us know what we would like to achieve with our lives. These are the big things in life. Unfortunately, as clear as these objectives may seem to us, at the end of the day, we really don't put in enough work to make those big goals happen sooner rather than later. That, in a nutshell, is our experience with focus.

How Important Is Focus?

Well, where your focus goes, your energy flows. The problem is, you only have so much energy to spare in any given day, week, month, or year. Not surprisingly, as clear as our "big goals" may be, they remain hopes and wishes. We lean back and think that these would be nice to accomplish, but we never get around to doing them.

The Challenge: There are so many things competing for and sucking up your personal focus that you have very little left for stuff that truly matters... Worst of all, the more you split up your focus, the less focus you have under your disposal.

How many times have you heard of people say that they can multitask? Well, don't fool yourself. Chances are, they are just fibbing. One of the dirty little secrets of personal productivity is that multitasking, in a large part, is a myth. Most people who try their hand at multitasking fail. This is due to the fact that you only have a set amount of focus every given day and if you divide that focus, the value of that focus is so low that you really don't accomplish much of anything. You've spread yourself too thin.

Take the case of a typical American worker. A person might put in 8 hours in the office, but I can guarantee you that in terms of work value, that typical employee's boss can probably count on maybe 1-2 hours of real work. The rest, you guessed it, is "fluff." We just end up chasing our tails and fail to accomplish much of anything worthwhile.

This book is written by Raza Imam and EAC Andrews, and we've discovered simple, actionable quick steps you can take to maximize your focus. In fact, we've created a 30-day plan for our focus-boosting system. Simply stick to this system and you'll be able to increase the amount of focus you have and maximize its effect. If you're struggling to achieve big goals, or you feel that you're not achieving stuff that truly matters, if you are feeling stuck in a familiar routine and can't seem to make a breakthrough, we have the solution for you.

This framework proceeds in a logical way: To maintain a high level of focus, you must first learn to build it up and learn to set the right goals to unleash your full potential.

These are all interrelated. You just have to take these sequential steps on a day to day basis. You start off with one focusing skill, and then you end the 30-day process with many more skills. This is an educational journey that engages you in a process that can end up transforming your personal power and focus. Using our system, every 3rd day, you will learn a new technique. The following day, you are given an opportunity to practice the technique you just learned.

This book is divided roughly into 3 groups of focus building skills:

- **Visualization**: The first group is visualization. These sets of skills help you increase your ability to focus on tasks and goals. You learn how to "get in the zone" when trying to achieve something. You'll also learn how to maximize the amount of willpower you have to tackle tasks in the quickest, most decisive, most effective, and most efficient way possible.

- **Goal Setting**: The next set of skills you would learn involve goal setting. These skills help you increase your chances of achieving the outcome you desire when you set goals. Believe it or not, most of us do have goals. The problem is, we set the wrong goals, or we go about setting them the wrong way, and this increases the likelihood that they will not pan out. This section helps you to set the right goals, sequence your goals for maximum power and focus, and scale up your goals to greater and greater results.

- **Maintaining Focus**: Finally, you will also learn skills that involve maintaining focus. These grab bags of skills help you continuously scale up the power and effectiveness of your personal focusing ability. Over these 30 days, you learn important techniques that enable you to sharpen your focus, boost your personal productivity, and increase the quality of the results you get from your actions.

Remember: The world doesn't care about your motivations or feelings. It couldn't care less. All it cares about is what you choose to do.

This system teaches you to ultimately change your behavior so you can change your world and reality. While there are some skills here that change your thinking, they are engineered to change your behavior because that is the only thing that the world recognizes. If you want to be successful, you have to produce results that the world needs and wants. They couldn't care less about your intentions, motivations or excuses. All it cares about is what you actually do.

This book is geared towards helping you produce the kind of results that will help you take your life to the next level. Stick to this program and you'll be able to focus at a very high level as a matter of habit. As the quote attributed to the great Chinese philosopher Confucius goes, if you sow a thought, you reap a word. If you sow a word, you reap an action. If you sow an action, you reap a habit. If you sow a habit, you reap a character. If you sow a character, you reap a destiny.

My friend, you are always in charge of your destiny based on your conscious thoughts. By buying this book, you have taken a concrete step toward living a life of unstoppable victory and success.
All the best,
Raza Imam & EAC Andrews

Day 1: Think BIG

"Decide upon your major definite purpose in life and then organize all your activities around it." – Brian Tracy

Identify Your 3 Biggest Objectives
For this day, I want you to think big. I want you to think way beyond what's in front of you. Focus on what you would like to do with your life. Now, this is a very open-ended question because there is no right answer. We all have different backgrounds, we come from different families, we have different experiences. It's really important to make sure that you are as clear as possible regarding the big objectives of your life.

Your objectives reflect your values. It reflects your character. It reflects what is truly important in your life. What may be important to one person may not be important to another person.

This is just the way it goes. Don't think that if certain values are important to your parents, it doesn't necessarily follow that it's important to you as well. This is why you need to be honest and dig deep and figure out what you really want to do with your life.

Now, fortunately, this type of question can only be asked if you ask another question which is, who am I? Now, it's really important to go through some soul searching because you might be living your life based on somebody else's agenda. You might be living your life based on somebody else's expectations. Now is the time to cut through the fluff, the self-deception, and the denial and to zero in on who you really are.

Once you figure out your real identity, you can then focus on what you would like to do with your life. At the end of the day, the only person whose happiness truly matters is yours. Not your parents, not the people "counting on you" or who have "invested" so much in you, but yourself. You have to come to this point, so ask yourself, what would you like to do with your life?

The next question is, why do you want to do these things? This question involves you identifying the payoffs that you think are most important to you. Some people are motivated by money. Other people are motivated by social status and external validation. Other people are driven by a sense of discovery. The good news is that there is no right or wrong answer because we're all different people. What's important is you identify your payoffs and your values.

What is most important to you? Is it the fact that people look up to you? Is it the fact that you have a lot of zeros at the end of a number in your bank account? Is it because of the fact that you can pick up and travel all over the world at the drop of a hat? What is most important to you? Unfortunately, we cannot hold your hand and guide you towards the right answer. There is no right answer because everybody is different. You have to figure this out yourself.

How Much Would You Give Up to Achieve These?

Now, after you've whipped out a piece of paper and wrote a lot of stuff and crossed out items while adding other items, you should have reached a point where you are clear as to what kind of things are very important to you. At this point, you haven't really ranked them. You haven't sorted them based on importance.

Now, I need you to ask yourself this question: How much would you give up to achieve these goals? This is all about sacrifice. How precious are your objectives that you would sacrifice present happiness, comfort, ease, money, status to achieve these objectives?

Reduce Your Big Objectives into the Top 3

According to a research study, human communication and focus are more powerful when people repeat things in 3's. Of course, this has a little bit of a cultural element to it because some cultures focus on the number 4, others on the number 7. Whatever the case may be, in the western tradition and psyche, the number 3 is particularly powerful. So we're going to use the power of 3 in terms of your objectives.

Now that you have listed all the things that you'd like to do in your life, and you have a rough idea of the things that you would give up for these things, the next step is to reduce that big list, as messy as it is, into the top 3. Now, again, there is no right answer here because everybody's goals are different. You have to just reach within and ask yourself, what's important to me now? What was important to me in the past, and what will continue to be important to me in the future? What's important here is to identify your classical needs.

Things that will remain true all throughout your life. This is the best way to filter what would otherwise be a confusing set of objectives.

Here's a hint. The 3 big objectives in your life should yield the most happiness, the greatest sense of accomplishment, and the most intense sense of meaning and purpose. According to the psychological theories of Abraham Maslow, the highest human need is not sex, food, shelter or power. Instead, the highest human need is the need for transcendence or meaning. Keep this in mind because a lot of the objectives in front of you might seem almost equally important. It can be very confusing because it seems that they are equal. But if you look at them from the perspective of purpose and meaning, it should clear up fairly quickly.

Another Hint
Keep in mind that these are not small victories. These are not mere strategic milestones. These big objectives that you select must define you. They must comprise a critical part of who you are as a person. When people look at you and realize what you have accomplished, they must be able to identify that objective with your values and, ultimately, your character.

This is a big deal. This is not like just figuring out how to create a better mousetrap, or getting a better job. That's just small potatoes if you think about it. Those are just empty details in the grand scheme of things. We're talking about the heavy stuff here. So, as you can probably already tell, this is not the kind of stuff that you are going to sit down at one time at a table at Starbucks and quickly figure out or rattle off the top of your head. No. It doesn't work that way.

You probably would have to go into Day 1 with a lot of the heavy lifting already out of your way. In other words, you already did some preliminary homework and Day 1 boils down to simply making a decision. Go through the sorting and filtration process again and again and again to make sure you've really zeroed in on your personal 3 big objectives.

I am emphatic that you do this because most people run after shadows. A lot of people define themselves based on their parent's values. A lot of people define themselves based on the expectation of the other people around them. While that, in and of itself, may not necessarily be bad, you have to remember that nobody else could live your life except you.

Nobody can be happy for you except you. This is why it's really important to go through that filtration process again and again until you're completely honest with yourself and can say to yourself that these are my 3 big objectives.

If you go through the process correctly, you have come up with something that is intimately personal to who you are. This is no time to be scared that your goals are somehow abnormal, weird, beyond the pale or unconventional. Let me be frank, who cares about what other people are thinking? It's not their life you're living, it's your life. Take ownership of your identity and make sure that you are completely honest with yourself. Otherwise, all that time, effort, sacrifice and focus would have been for nothing.

Your Biggest Drivers

At this point in the process, you probably should have invested quite a bit of time figuring out what your 3 biggest objectives are. Keep in mind that these will become your biggest drivers. Your pursuit of these 3 big goals provides you with purpose, stoke your personal passion, and stir your personal creativity.

It's very hard to fight a battle that you don't believe in. Maybe the money will be enough to motivate you in the beginning, but lust for money eventually dies down. Maybe it's the idealism that pushes you forward the first few weeks, but even that has its limits. You have to be completely honest with yourself so you can remain engaged by your 3 big objectives regardless of the frustration, failure, misery and even outright opposition that you face from other people.

Success is never easy. If it was, then all of us would be extremely successful in our own way, but we're not. Most of us are frustrated. Most of us are feeling stuck. Most of us are feeling like we're living life at a level that is way below our fullest potential.

You're going to go on a journey that will go against all of that. You will not be mediocre. You will not take things for how they are. You will not go along to get along. You're going to swing for the fences, and this process requires that you have the purpose, the passion and the drive to muster all your personal creativity and tap into your unlimited personal imagination to turn these 3 big objectives into reality.

It takes a lot to see the world with eyes of faith because the world would tell you that you are stuck where you are. Things will not change. Things will only get worse. Well, I've got some good news for you. If Gandhi and Steve Jobs thought that way, the world would be a much more miserable place. Thankfully, there are people who got past the programming.

This is the day you are going to turn the power of objective identification to your favor. You can turn things that you have previously hoped and wished for into things that you can actually see, touch, taste, hear and smell. In other words, you can turn ideas into reality. Now is your moment to do that. Give yourself the time and the space to make that happen. You have to write down your 3 biggest life objectives.

Day 2: Practice

Practice Day 1's Technique

For Day 2, go through the information we provided on Day 1 and practice them. There's a lot to chew on. It's not as easy as you think. It's not as clear cut. Why? A lot of the things that you think are very important to you may not turn out to be all that substantial. If you allow yourself to be completely honest and deprogram yourself from the influence of other people, it may be quite scary because you are walking in virgin territory. But you need to do this.

So Day 2 is all about revisiting whatever breakthroughs you've experienced on Day 1, and retesting them. Again, give yourself enough time. If it takes 8 hours, so be it. If it takes 16 hours, be prepared to do that. What matters is that you put in the time, effort and energy to make sure that you are zeroing in, honestly, on the 3 big objectives that will push your life forward.

Practice:
Thinking Big

Day 3: Figure Out What You Want

"My main focus is on my game" – Tiger Woods

Set Up Goals that Lead You to Big Wins

Now that you have identified your 3 big life objectives, this is where things get more practical as far as your day to day activities go. While your big objectives are ultimate life destinations, for Day 3, you're going to focus on how to plan your actions in a systematic and methodical way so you get from point a to point b as far as goal attainment is concerned. If you think that your grand life objectives are just floating out in the distant horizon somewhere, they will remain distant. You will never be able to achieve them because, ultimately, you are treating them like fantasies. You need to stop thinking along those lines by using solid goal setting techniques. Here are the steps that you need to follow:

Step #1: Break Up Your 3 Big Objectives into a Series of Goals

When you look at a big objective, you'll realize that it's actually made up of many different goals. For example, if your ultimate objective is to become a senior partner at the top litigation law firm in your city, and you're still in college, you would realize that there is a lot in between where you are currently and where you need to go. At the very least, you need to take the LSAT, law school aptitude test in most jurisdictions in the United States. You need to get a high enough score so you can get into a law school that is prestigious enough to open doors for you as far as law firms go. You probably would need to spend several years as a junior associate at a prestigious Washington, DC or Wall Street or possibly Los Angeles law firm to get the prestige you need to then come back to your hometown or home city and take your pick of the top firms there. Once you go through that process, you should be positioned on the fast track to becoming a senior partner sooner rather than later. Do you see how this works?

There are a lot of things that need to happen in each of those steps, and each of those steps can be broken down into goals. For example, taking the LSAT and you're in college, maybe you're a sophomore. Well, at this stage, the best thing you can do is to take practice tests over and over again. It's a good idea to use flashcards and diagrams to quickly wrap your mind around logic games. Historically speaking, these have been the most difficult parts of the LSAT. Most people can deal quite well with reading and comprehension questions as well as simple reasoning. However, most people stumble with logic games.

If you give yourself a two year head start for visually diagramming what would otherwise be mind-numbingly complex logic games, this can possibly become second nature to you so you do well on the LSAT. Also, at this point in your academic career, you could also join all sorts of clubs and participate in volunteer organizations so you can have something interesting to say in your law school personal statement or application essay. Do you see how this all works out? A lot of planning has to happen now. You then have to take those sub-goals and deliver on them so they can yield higher goals, which ultimately, lead to your final objective.

Step #2: Break Up Each Goal Into Subgoals

In the case of the law firm example mentioned above, I already identified big goals that need to happen.

To recap, you need to get a high score on the LSAT, get accepted into the right law schools, get into the right law firms, and then get hired by the right local firms. These are dependent on each other. There is a chronological sequence to them. You then break up each big goal, for example, scoring very high on the LSAT, and you turn that into subgoals.

How exactly do you score as close to 180 on the LSAT? Very simple, you prepare early. Like I said before, maybe you're a sophomore now, it's never too early to start taking LSAT practice exams. You can order these online, you can also look at derivative exams available on the internet. Whatever the case is, train yourself to take these tests again and again and again. Ultimately, you would be able to finish them on time, and also not be intimidated by them. That's the key.

A lot of people say that a particular test, whether it's the GMAT to get into MBA schools, or the MCAT to get into medical school, are difficult tests. What they're really saying is that they didn't prepare. Because if you prepare for anything, a lot of the intimidation goes away. It becomes second nature. You start picking up on certain things and recognizing them and that level of comfort ensures you don't choke.

Believe it or not, most of the people who score really low on standardized tests are not idiots. Instead, they choked. They got intimidated by the test because something that they could have tackled easily came wrapped in clothing that they did not recognize. By practicing early, you can destroy that intimidation. You would be more at ease and chances are quite good that you would perform at a peak level. The way to do this, of course, is to break up each big goal into subgoals.

Step #3: Apply a Timeline to Each Sub-goal

Now that you have a clear understanding of the sub-goals you need to reach big goals, apply a realistic timeline. The keyword here is realistic. Don't think that you are smarter than you really are. Don't think that you're more efficient than you really are. This is not an exercise in wishful thinking. Instead, focus on who you really are, what you're capable of in the here and now. Give yourself a realistic timeline.

Now, a realistic timeline doesn't mean that you're going to stretch out the timeline as far as humanly possible. That's not much of a timeline because the whole point of any kind of deadline is to force you to act.

It's a forcing mechanism. If you stretch the deadline too liberally, you don't feel forced. There's no sense of urgency and as a result, you probably will cram and end up where you began.

The whole point of advance preparation is to gain a competitive advantage. That's not going to happen if your timelines are too liberal. You need to feel the heat. You need to feel some sort of pressure so you can push yourself to ever-increasing levels of effort.

Step #4: Create a Schedule of To-Do Lists for Each Sub-goal

Now that you have a timeline for your sub-goals, there are daily things that you can do to achieve those sub-goals. Maybe you're working your way towards those sub-goals and taking care of small tasks, or you are taking care of preparatory steps and those lead you closer and closer to your sub-goals. Whatever the case may be, create to-do lists every month for your sub-goals and then break them down into weekly to-do lists, and then break those down into daily to-do lists.

It's important to note here that there is no such thing as an impossible goal. Believe it or not, before the US space shuttle started making regular trips to space, a lot of people thought that was just impossible because rocket technology hasn't advanced to a certain point. But the United States was able to do it. Why? They had the right goals and the right timelines. You have to set the right timelines and you would realize that there is no such thing as an impossible goal. You have to set up goals with timelines that will not rob you of your focus and energy.

By breaking big objectives into goals and sub-goals, you can clearly see the stuff that you can do today that will then ultimately lead to you achieving your big dreams. You feel that it is possible, you feel a tremendous level of control over your actions because if you do stuff today, ultimately, it leads to something big that you would like to achieve in the future. Now, it's important to keep in mind that when you break up big goals into smaller and manageable chunks, they become more realistic and more probable and more realizable. Compare this with failing to break them up into subgoals and simply allowing yourself to be intimidated by your big objective. You can bet that it would be intimidating because there is really no logical chain of actions that look probable between where you are now, and where you need to go.

For example, the US moon mission looked impossible during the time of President John F. Kennedy. Afterall, they only had rockets, but nobody had been to the moon. Not even close. What made it possible was that they broke up the science and logistics of getting to the moon in small, easy to manage parts and they applied a timeline to it. A few short years later, Neil Armstrong was on the moon. That's how powerful effective goal setting can be.

Day #4: Practice

For this day, wrap your mind around the goal setting techniques outlined in Day 3. Slice and dice the information and see if you have broken down your big goals into modular enough parts. Also, double-check if the timeline that you have selected for achieving those big objectives are realistic. By realistic, I am of course talking about being realistic in terms of your present resources as well as probable resources in the near future.

It's also important to make sure that you break down everything into detailed enough steps so that there are no missing steps. You don't want to set up a plan where there are tremendous leaps of faith from one point to the next. That's not a goal. That's not effective goal setting. Instead, you're just engaged in fantasy or wishful thinking. I hope you can see the difference. Real goal setting involves practical steps from now and working with the things you can see to the things you cannot see and there are clear and probable steps to that goal.

Practice:
Thinking about big objectives in your life
Figuring out specifically what you want to achieve those big objectives

Day #5: Be RUTHLESS With Your Time

"It is not enough to be busy; so are the ants.
The question is: what are we busy about?"
– Henry David Thoreau

Strip Your To-Do List into Top 3 Daily Tasks
Now that you have a set of to-do lists, the next step is to strip them down based on your ability to make them happen. This is really important because a lot of people create to-do lists and they end up intimidating themselves. It is not an accident when you start out the day with a to-do list and never get around to achieving much of anything. The reason why this happens is you psychologically sabotage yourself. You end up doing a lot of the stuff that doesn't really add much as far as your goals go and have very little focus left over for the things that do count.

41

The steps below will help you practice better to-do list management. It really all boils down to proper management.

Step #1: Understand the 80/20 Rule

The 80/20 rule, also known as the Pareto Principle, states that 20% of the things that you do account for 80% of your results. It logically follows that you should take that 20% and stretch it to 100%. In other words, get rid of the stuff that really doesn't add much to the bottom line as far as your to-do lists are concerned. This should be your goal. Apply that 80/20 rule to how you manage your to-do lists.

Step #2: Use the 80/20 Rule to Mercilessly Simplify Your Daily Tasks

This is where a little bit of emotional and intellectual courage comes in. If you are like most Americans, you're probably thinking that you need to do all these things because you might lose control. Believe me, I fully understand where you're coming from. It's easy to get emotionally connected to your to-do list, but if you want to be successful and nail your to-do list day in, day out like a machine, you need to let go.

This is where things get real. You need to look at your to-do list and apply the 80/20 rule. Ask yourself which 3 items lead to the most results. "Most results" in this context, of course, means that they bring you the closest to your goal, which then brings you to your big goal. You'd be surprised at the results. You'd be surprised to learn that the vast majority of the stuff that you do every single day, don't really add up too much

For example, checking Facebook, screwing around with email, doing "research" on Google. In many cases, you don't have anything to do with your big objectives, much less your goals. Apply the 80/20 rule mercilessly to the things that you do on a typical day and you'd be surprised as to what you'll find. You'll be both scared and emboldened by the fact that there is 20% that you can stretch for maximum results.

Step #3: Prioritize Tasks and Break Them Up into Top 3 Tasks

Now that you have applied the 80/20 filter to the things that you do, you need to decide which are the top 3 tasks that would produce the most results. Again, this will take quite a bit of courage and you would have to learn how to let go, but believe me, this pays off tremendously.

Step #4: For Everything Else: Practice DOI

DOI stands for delegate, outsource, or ignore. Look at the rest of the stuff on your list and ask yourself, can this be delegated? If so, how much money is involved? Can this be outsourced? If so, who should I outsource it to and how much do I have to spend?

Finally, look at the stuff that can be safely ignored. This is stuff that really doesn't bring anything substantive to the table. Sure it makes you feel good, sure they bring a lot of enjoyment, but when it comes to actively working on your big 3 objectives, they really don't add much. So do yourself a big favor and ignore these for your working hours. This doesn't mean that you have to completely shut them out of your life. You can still do them during your leisure time or your off days, but make sure they never creep back into your productive days.

Day 6: Practice

Practice Day 5's techniques along with all the other techniques learned from previous days. It's important to revisit the goal-setting skill you learned on Day 3 as well as keeping a laser focus on the revelation made possible by Day 1. Make sure that you are constantly going back to these previous techniques.

Remember, the whole point of this book is to give you the skills that you need to maximize your focus. It's not going to happen if you look at each succeeding day as essentially divorced or disconnected from the other days. They have to feed into each other. They have to empower each other.

Think of it like going up a staircase. You can only go up to the next level if you're standing on a level that rests on the previous level. As far as building up your personal focus goes, this requires constantly referring back to what you learned previously on Day 5.

Practice:

- Thinking about big objectives in your life
- Figuring out specifically what you want to achieve those big objectives
- Ruthless cut out "fluff" tasks and focus on the main items to achieve your goals – delegate everything else

Day 7: See With Your "Mind's Eye"

"The indispensable first step to getting things you want out of life is this; decide what you want"

-Ben Stein

If you learn and practice sensory visualization to achieve anything worthwhile in life, you have to remain motivated while you pursue your goals. Otherwise, you're going to get sidetracked. Otherwise, you're going to get confused, and all of a sudden, years pass by and you never end up achieving the life that you originally had dreamed of.

If you ask most middle-aged men in the United States what their big goals when they were in their early 20's were, I can guarantee you that in the majority of cases, the reality they're living now doesn't match their earlier goals. In other words, their early hopes and dreams were dashed.

They never got around to achieving them. I don't want that to happen to you. You need to find a focus that you need to keep going until you hit your top 3 objectives. These are the big objectives of your life.

Unfortunately, this is easier said than done because life is very complicated. As the old saying goes, life is what happens when you're making other plans. In your 20's you may have everything all figured out and you're definitely welcome to feel that way. However, once you get married, you have a kid, and you work your first corporate job, things have a way of just spiraling out of control and then you wake up as a middle-aged person asking yourself, "What did I do with my life?"

This may sound like the typical midlife crisis, but believe it or not, midlife crises happen during your mid 30's, mid 20's. It can even while you're in college. You need to understand how this plays out. And the best way to avoid this is to make sure you have the proper focus in the here and now to continue to go after your to-do lists day in and day out until you achieve your sub-goals and then keep pushing forward until you achieve goals, and then ultimately, you should have knocked out enough goals to achieve your big objectives. That's how it works.

As you can probably see how I described this process, it's a marathon, not a sprint. It's not one of those things that you just do one day and all of a sudden you are assured a tremendous future. It doesn't work that way. Real success involves struggling day after day to find the energy and the focus to do what you need to do to knock out that to-do list day after day, week after week, month after month, year after year.

It can get very tiring. It's not uncommon for many people to just wake up one day and say, "What the hell am I doing?" You need to resist all of that. You need to make it through. You need to find an internal power source that enables you to do whatever is needed for however long until you achieve the big victories you're craving for in your life.

Visualization is crucial to all of that because it gives you the skill to develop an internal power source. Remember, you cannot depend on other people. People change overnight. You cannot depend on the right circumstances happening to you. This is really a fancy way of saying you cannot depend on being lucky. The only person you can depend on is yourself and you have to find that power within you.

This is why visualization is so powerful. It is essential. If you were to interview a lot of successful people, you would realize that a lot of them have rituals.

A lot of them have a certain way of thinking. They were able to do this because of a certain mental focus based on skill. The skill I will teach you below enables you to develop that inner source of urgency so you can develop a high level of personal focus.

Set aside 15 minutes at the beginning of the day, and at the end of the day. Make sure you have a quiet room you can spend time in. Also, make sure that when you're in that quiet room, you spend it alone.

There are no distractions, there are no people talking to you, there is nobody else making demands on you. This is serious alone time. The good news is that, all told, it only takes 2 15-minute blocks. As much as possible, try to do this for more than 15 minutes, but you can still achieve great results with a minimum of 15 minutes.

Here are the steps:

Step #1: Remember Your 3 Big Life Objectives

The first thing that you need to do is zero in on why you are doing all this. Zero in on your 3 big life objectives. These are the things that you are basing your life around. These are the things that you're chasing for with your time, effort, energy and personal focus. Remember them. List them out in your mind.

Step #2: Remember Why They're Important

It's one thing to think of things on an intellectual level. The problem with an intellectual acceptance of personal truths is that they're not real enough. Human beings are emotional creatures and things are only real to us if they hit an emotional reality. Still, you need to flat-out list the reasons off the top of your head why these 3 big life objectives are so important. A good question to ask is what makes these so much more important than other potential life objectives. You need to come up with clear answers to yourself.

Step#3: Imagine Yourself Achieving These 3 Big Life Objectives

Going back to that law firm example, imagine yourself being named by the senior partner at your big local firm that you are now a senior partner. Imagine the details of the scene. What would that person look like? How would it feel to walk up to that person's office? Can you imagine the point where that person said that now you will be making a certain percentage of the firm's earnings, which can mean several million dollars every single year? What kind of mental pictures can you come up with? Can you remember the scene? What do people look like in that mental image? What would the rooms and furniture look like?

Step #4: "Recreate" Sensory Signals

It's one thing to imagine yourself at a different place and time. Most people are able to do that. I mean, if you pick up a book, you can easily fantasize that you are front and center of the action right next to Frodo in Lord of the Rings. Most people could do that. The problem is, when you're imagining things this way, you're doing things on a purely intellectual level.

As I mentioned above, if you approach things on a purely intellectual level, it is not real enough. For it to be real, you have to approach it with your heart. It has to be emotionally real.

The best way to do this in sensory visualization is to "recreate" sights, sounds, textures, smells, and tastes. In other words, breathe into and imagine as much detail into the point in the future where you gain your big life objective.

Going back to the law firm example, what would the room smell like? What would the senior partner's room smell like when he is saying to you that you are now a senior partner in the top law firm in your city? Can you taste what's in your mouth as you anticipate the words coming out of his mouth and you feel the rush of energy? Can you feel your heart beating within you knowing full well that you have reached the defining point of your legal career? Can you imagine the words leaving his mouth and what emotions those words trigger?

Step #5: Imaging How it Would Feel

Now, the whole point of Step #4 is to set up enough sensory triggers so that you achieve some sort of emotional reaction. Just as no piece of music is emotionally neutral, no imagined sensory stimulation is emotionally neutral. There will be an emotional reaction. The key is to make it as vividly as possible. So make sure that when you close your eyes and practice sensory visualization.

The sights are crisp, the sounds are believable, the textures are as expected, and the smells and tastes all lead to some sort of realistic picture. The more you can sense these different details, the higher the likelihood that your visualized scene will produce an emotional reality.

Step #6: Freeze the Main Emotions Behind the Accomplishment

Now that you're going through these scenes repeatedly in your head for 15 minutes, you are probably feeling all sorts of emotions. That's perfectly normal, but I need you to zero in on the most intense emotion that you're feeling.

Again, with the law firm example, you probably would be feeling a tremendous amount of gratitude, relief, a sense of a job well done, and a sense that you have achieved something with your life. It's a victory that nobody can take away from you. It's a victory that nobody can diminish and say you owe it to your father or you owe it to blind luck. No, it's something that you yourself worked hard for and achieved.

I need you to freeze those emotions and sear them into your emotional memory bank. During the first few times, this is probably not going to be very easy for you to do. However, you do have Day 8 to keep practicing this again, along with other skills. You need to keep practicing this until it becomes seared into your emotional memory and you can call it into action very easily.

Day 8: Practice

Practice Day 7's technique, along with all other techniques learned from previous days. You have the whole day to keep practicing these and applying them to your to-do tasks.

Day 7 is an important milestone because you learned how to create an emotional power source within you. This power source gives you a tremendous amount of drive. You can then start focusing this drive on the daily to-do tasks that you need to do every single day.

Practice:

- **Think Big**: Thinking about big objectives in your life
- **Set Specific Goals**: Figuring out specifically what you want to achieve those big objectives
- **Be Ruthless With Your Time**: Ruthless cut out "fluff" tasks and focus on the main items to achieve your goals — delegate everything else

- **See With Your Mind's Eye**: Visualize yourself having already accomplished your goals. Feel the excitement, passion, and confidence you would feel.

Day 9: The "Rip Your Goals" Ritual

"Concentration is the secret of strengths in politics, in war, in trade, in short in all management of human affairs"
– Ralph Waldo Emerson

Erase and write down your big 3 objectives daily. Up to this point in time, your big 3 objectives are things that you wrote down in the past and you consciously remember every single day.

Now, going forward, you will be using a specific ritual that enables you to remain emotionally engaged by your big 3 objectives. This technique is quite simple, but it's also very powerful.

Step #1: Remember the Big 3 Objectives You Identified on Day 1

The first thing that you need to do is simply remember them. By this point, you should be able to do this easily because you've been at it for several days now.

Step #2: Write Them Down

At this point you will just be hanging on to your big objectives on a purely mental level. Starting today, you have to physically whip out a piece of paper, grab a pen and write down your big 3 objectives. It's important that you do this slowly. Feel the words materialize as you write them down. Whether you write in cursive or printed out, it doesn't matter. What matters is you pay close attention as you write down each word of your 3 big objectives.

Step #3: Read Them Slowly

Now that you've written down your big 3 objectives, the next step is to read them slowly. Don't read them to yourself. Read them out loud. Now, if you're at Starbucks or in public, this might make you look foolish but you shouldn't care. This is more important than what other people that you don't know think about you. This is all about personal power.

In fact, the more awkward you feel in a social setting, the more powerful this technique would be. Why? There is some sort of social shame factor that is pushing you to feel the range of emotions you need to feel to stay focused on your big 3 objectives.

So read them out loud, slowly, and make sure you read them carefully. Pay attention to each word. Pay attention to the meaning of each word. Be aware of the different meanings of each word and zero in on the meaning that you want for each goal.

Step #4: Rip Up the Paper and Write Them Again

At this stage, writing down your goal should have had some sort of emotional effect on you. In the beginning, the effect is not as intense as you probably desired. That's okay because you're going to rip up the paper and write them again. That's right, you're going through the same process again.

Step #5: Write Your Big Goals Down, Rip Up the Paper, and Write Them Again

All told, you should have gone through this ritual 3 different times. This is the power of 3 working on your life. Make sure that you go through the process carefully. Read them carefully, write slowly, read them out loud. When you're going through this process, this is not some empty, meaningless ritual.

This is not like some obligatory list of empty actions that don't really mean much of anything. No. What you're doing is you are engaging your physical body with your mind, and you refocus your consciousness to the 3 big objectives of your life. After enough repetition, this prevents you from acting in a directionless way. You are constantly reminded, both from conscious and subconscious processes of the 3 objectives guiding, shaping, and informing your life. What you're doing is mental reprogramming.

Believe it or not, there's not much difference between you and Bill Gates in terms of physical capability. You have the same hardware. The reason why Bill Gates is worth northwards of $80 billion is that he chose to program his mind with a different operating system. The reason why you are achieving whatever it is that you're achieving previously is because of the software that you have chosen. The good news is that you can deprogram yourself and reprogram yourself using the steps I outlined above.

Day 10: Practice

Practice Day 9's techniques along with all the other techniques learned from previous days. Keep repeating them until they become second nature to you. Your end goal is to develop them into habits. You have to have a habitual manner of thinking, a habitual manner of speaking, a habitual manner of looking at things. The good news is, success is a habit. It's a collection of mindsets that you pick up. The good news is that you can choose certain habits and choose to unlearn or get rid of others.

Practice:
- **Think Big**: Thinking about big objectives in your life
- **Set Specific Goals**: Figuring out specifically what you want to achieve those big objectives
- **Be Ruthless With Your Time**: Ruthless cut out "fluff" tasks and focus on the main items to achieve your goals – delegate everything else

- **See With Your Mind's Eye**: Visualize yourself having already accomplished your goals. Feel the excitement, passion, and confidence you would feel.
- **Rip Your Goals**: You want to have an emotional response to your goals. Writing and re-reading them is part of that. Ripping them and writing them again reinforces the desire, passion, and zeal you have toward your goals. You want to create as much emotion around them as possible – and of course, focus those emotions into action.

Day 11: Be Comfortable With Discomfort

"If a man does not know to what port he is steering, no wind is favorable to him"
-Seneca

Wake up early and take a cold shower. This may be a simple ritual, but it's extremely powerful. You have to adopt a new habit that centers your physical focus on the day ahead. If you take a shower late in the day, you're not giving your emotional state enough of a physical jolt to get going. When you wake up early, let's say 5 o'clock or even 4 in the morning, you adopt a new habit that enables you to physically focus on the day ahead.

Your physical asset is primed for the day ahead. The cold shower wakes you up. Your focus is woken up because of the cold temperature and this sharpened focus enables you to achieve more with your day. Compare this with just lounging around and allowing your energy levels to deplete along with your focus throughout the rest of your day, there is no comparison.

Another reason why you should wake up early and take a cold shower is so you change your body's schedule to focus most of your energy to the early and middle parts of your day. According to several research studies, these are the parts of the day where most people are productive. By jolting yourself with a cold shower as early as possible in the day, you train your mind and focus all its firepower and energy to the early and middle part of your day.

Day 12: Practice

Practice Day 11's techniques along with all the other previous day's techniques. Every other day is your practice day. The good news is, the more you practice, the better you get at them, also, the less time they take. The key here is not just to go through the motions. The key is to turn these into habits.

Practice:

- **Think Big**: Thinking about big objectives in your life
- **Set Specific Goals**: Figuring out specifically what you want to achieve those big objectives
- **Be Ruthless With Your Time**: Ruthless cut out "fluff" tasks and focus on the main items to achieve your goals – delegate everything else
- **See With Your Mind's Eye**: Visualize yourself having already accomplished your goals. Feel the excitement, passion, and confidence you would feel.

- **Rip Your Goals**: You want to have an emotional response to your goals. Writing and re-reading them is part of that. Ripping them and writing them again reinforces the desire, passion, and zeal you have toward your goals. You want to create as much emotion around them as possible – and of course focus those emotions into action.

- **Get Comfortable Being Uncomfortable**: You need to get comfortable being uncomfortable. This will teach you to focus your energy and attention on your goals. Some examples are to start waking up earlier, take cold showers, resisting junk food, etc. The main point is to be conscious that you are doing this to develop focus and discipline; NOT to punish yourself. View it as sharpening yourself, not wearing yourself down.

Day 13: Create "Layers" of Focus

"Lack of direction, not time, is the problem. We all have 24-hour days"
–Zig Ziglar

"Layer" your to-do list. Most people have a tough time knocking out their to-do lists simply because they set up their to-do list to rob them of their focus. They get intimidated, they end up burning out too early in the day and then they end up unable to do much of anything with the rest of the day. It's important to layer your to-do list in such a way that your focus is preserved throughout the day. Of course, you know full well that the crucial stuff on your to-do list is going to suck up your focus until you just have enough to finish the last task at the end of the day.

But unfortunately, most people don't get around to doing this. In many cases, the first item or the first two items are so formidable and so intimidating that they don't have any focus left to take care of the third item. Currently, your to-do list is filled with must-do "crucial stuff." You have to power through them or else your day is not complete. This can be very tiring because it depletes your focus. You end up feeling frustrated.

For Day 13, you're going to learn how to schedule your to-do lists so you conserve your focus and maximize it to knock out your complete to-do list. Here's how you do it:

Step #1: Identify the 3 Simplified but Hardest Stuff You Have to Achieve Today

These are the simplified steps that you need to knock out today. These must lead to your big 3 objectives. This must be very clear. Sure, they may lead to a Sub-goal, which can lead to a goal, which then leads to the big stuff. Regardless, you need to be able to trace a straight line from the crucial stuff you need to do now to the big things in life you want to accomplish.

Step #2: Sandwich Ministerial or Housekeeping Stuff in Between the Hardest Items

On your to-do list, there must be 3 hardest items. These are the things that are absolutely crucial to eventually get you to your big 3 objectives. In between these, include ministerial stuff. This is stuff that doesn't take much effort or thinking on your part. What you're trying to do is you knock out a hard item and you quickly burn through an easy item, and then you do another hard item.

Step #3: Work Through Your List of Items

Why should you do things this way? Well, by switching from "hard" to "easy" and back to "hard" again, you don't end up depleting your will power. In fact, the sense of accomplishment you feel when you knock out a hard item followed up by an easy to do item "recharges" your focus so you can then knock out another difficult item. Of course, I don't expect you to do this easily the first time you try it. However, this book is all about teaching you new habits. If you keep practicing this day in and day out, this will become second nature to you and you would be able to burn through all your to-do list items day after day.

Day 14: Practice

Practice Day 13's techniques along your other previously learned techniques. Again, focus on creating efficiency. Try to do previous techniques faster. Try to achieve a higher degree of emotional urgency from them. As you go along, the techniques you learn from previous days take less and less time, but their impact on your focus increases over time.

Practice:

- **Think Big**: Thinking about big objectives in your life
- **Set Specific Goals**: Figuring out specifically what you want to achieve those big objectives
- **Be Ruthless With Your Time**: Ruthless cut out "fluff" tasks and focus on the main items to achieve your goals – delegate everything else

- **See With Your Mind's Eye**: Visualize yourself having already accomplished your goals. Feel the excitement, passion, and confidence you would feel.

- **Rip Your Goals**: You want to have an emotional response to your goals. Writing and re-reading them is part of that. Ripping them and writing them again reinforces the desire, passion, and zeal you have toward your goals. You want to create as much emotion around them as possible – and of course, focus those emotions into action.

- **Get Comfortable Being Uncomfortable**: You need to get comfortable being uncomfortable. This will teach you to focus your energy and attention on your goals. Some examples are to start waking up earlier, take cold showers, resisting junk food, etc. The main point is to be conscious that you are doing this to develop focus and discipline; NOT to punish yourself. View it as sharpening yourself, not wearing yourself down.

- **Layers of Focus**: Do the hard stuff and follow it up with easy stuff. The feeling of accomplishment and confidence will enhance your focus – not deplete it.

Day 15: Sleep More, Eat Less

"It is during our darkest moments that we must
focus to see the light"
–Aristotle Onasiss

Go to bed early and practice intermittent fasting

Fasting usually scares most people. Give up food to achieve more focus and discipline?! Are you crazy? Well, believe it or not, you're already fasting. Usually, when people think of fasting, they think of some monk that goes up on a mountain somewhere and doesn't eat for 100 days, to pick a round number. They think of it as some sort of self-punishment or involving some sort of misery.

Well, believe it or not, you're already fasting. Fasting, as technically defined, is a period of time where you're not eating. In any 24-hour period, you're not eating when you're sleeping.

Intermittent fasting is all about stretching the window of time in any 24-hour period where you're not eating and you're doing something else. It starts with the 6-8 hours you're sleeping and then you add on several hours where you're not eating.

Why should you practice intermittent fasting? What does this have to do with building focus? Well, the more you can control your body, the more you can control your focus. If you spend most of your waking hours thinking about your next meal or eating at your favorite restaurant, your focus gets depleted.

You start thinking less of the hard stuff you need to knock out and you start thinking more about your next meal. If this becomes a habit, then you essentially rob yourself of focus at key parts of your day.

By practicing intermittent fasting, you get off on the wrong track. You instead preserve your focus on where it needs to go. Follow the steps below to adopt intermittent fasting and maximize its impact on your focus.

Step #1: Go to Bed 1 Hour Earlier Than Usual

This should be self-explanatory. Make yourself go to bed 1 hour earlier than usual. This can take some doing because we're creatures of habit, but the more you do this, the better you will get at it.

Step #2: Restrict Your Meals to an 8-Hour Window

This 8-hour window is either immediately after you wake up, meaning this is your breakfast and lunchtime, or it's 8 hours before you go to bed. In other words, we're talking about eating lunch as your first meal of the day and then eating dinner. I'm giving you some flexibility in scheduling because different people have different preferences. Some people are breakfast people, other people are more lunch people, while others prefer a nice dinner. Whatever the case may be, just stick to that 8-hour window where you allow yourself to eat.

Step #3: After You Get Used to Your New Sleeping Schedule, Sleep 1 Hour Earlier

Now that you have gotten to the practice of sleeping 1 hour earlier, scale things up by sleeping 1 hour earlier. The good news is this can be done.

As long as you have repeated this several times before, it becomes easier and easier to do.

Step #4: Restrict Your Meals to a 7-hour Window

Your mealtime is also going to face pressure. You start out with 8 and then now you're going to shrink it down to 7 hours where you're eating. It doesn't really matter whether it's after you wake up or before you go to sleep, as long as you stick to eating at that 7-hour window, you will achieve progress.

Keep repeating this process until you restrict your meals to a 4-6 hour window. Do not eat outside this window. The happy byproduct of this focus-building technique is that it enables you to lose weight. It's very easy to lose weight using this process. In fact, intermittent fasting is one of the hottest trends among bodybuilders now because it's so powerful, effective, and, if you have the right mental focus, quite easy. But in addition to the physical benefits, it also does great wonders to your ability to focus.

If you go from somebody who's just constantly thinking of your next meal to focusing on a 4-6 hour window where you can eat, you develop a tremendous sense of discipline. This enables you to focus on what you need to do for the rest of your day. You build discipline and, most importantly, this ability to focus on this short time frame where you can eat, taps into your personal momentum because the moment you change your eating habits, it's only a matter of time until they pretty much change for good. It can take some time to achieve great progress, but once you get started, it becomes a habit.

Day 16: Practice

Practice Day 15's technique along with all previous techniques. By this point, you should have gotten really efficient with earlier techniques. Most of your focus should go into becoming more efficient with more recent days' techniques.

Practice:

- **Think Big**: Thinking about big objectives in your life
- **Set Specific Goals**: Figuring out specifically what you want to achieve those big objectives
- **Be Ruthless With Your Time**: Ruthless cut out "fluff" tasks and focus on the main items to achieve your goals – delegate everything else
- **See With Your Mind's Eye**: Visualize yourself having already accomplished your goals. Feel the excitement, passion, and confidence you would feel.
- **Rip Your Goals**: You want to have an emotional response to your goals. Writing

and re-reading them is part of that. Ripping them and writing them again reinforces the desire, passion, and zeal you have toward your goals. You want to create as much emotion around them as possible – and of course, focus those emotions into action.

- **Get Comfortable Being Uncomfortable**: You need to get comfortable being uncomfortable. This will teach you to focus your energy and attention on your goals. Some examples are to start waking up earlier, take cold showers, resisting junk food, etc. The main point is to be conscious that you are doing this to develop focus and discipline; NOT to punish yourself. View it as sharpening yourself, not wearing yourself down.

- **Create "Layers" of Focus**: Do the hard stuff and follow it up with easy stuff. The feeling of accomplishment and confidence will enhance your focus – not deplete it.

- **Sleep More, Eat Less**: Most of us eat too much and sleep too little. Focus on getting 7-8 hours of sleep and focusing on eating better. Be mindful when you eat, appreciate the flavors, chew slowly, enjoy your food. Eating more mindfully and sleeping more soundly will help sharpen your focus.

Day 17: F#*k Facebook

"Concentrate all your thoughts upon the work at hand. The sun's rays do not until brought to a focus"
–Alexander Graham Bell

Seriously, is that more important than the goal you're trying to achieve? Sure, it's fun to read, but is it helping you accomplish your goals?

Preserve your willpower by restricting email and social media update checks.

Believe it or not, when you check your email or check for social media updates on Facebook, Twitter, and what have you. You end up burning through quite a bit of your personal willpower. How come?

Well, any activity that involves any kind of analysis, decision making, or choosing, necessarily burns willpower. This is a lesson that Steve Jobs of Apple computer fame learned early on. Why do you think he keeps wearing the same turtleneck outfit? Why do you think he tends to stick to the same wardrobe regardless of how many billions he is worth.

Believe me, it's not because he can't afford Giorgio Armani threads. Nope. He knows full well that the more thought he puts into making what would otherwise be trivial decisions robs him of the willpower he needs for the stuff that truly matters.

You can learn a thing or two, from how Steve Jobs operated by clearly limiting the time you spent checking email or getting updated on social media. While this doesn't necessarily mean that you have to cut these activities out of your average day entirely, what it does mean is that you can safely segregate these activities on your schedule to maximize your remaining willpower.

Personally, I would reserve the first few hours for pure work. I would do nothing else and think of nothing else except work. This is hard stuff. This is the stuff that burns a lot of willpower.

Once done with those, however, and have gotten one or a couple of big things out of the way, I would then budget maybe 30 minutes of my time to check email, or look up updates and status on Facebook, and other social media accounts.

The secret here is not the amount of time you budget to yourself. You can keep things down to 15 minutes. You can even do 30 minutes. What matters is not the duration but your consistency.

In other words, put simply, if you decide to budget 30 minutes, stick to it. I have seen it happen to even the very best and most focused people where they would start with 15 minutes of email and then this would grow slowly but decisively into 30 minutes, and then an hour, and then two hours. By the time they're done, they basically are back to their old work habits.

There is a reason why the vast majority of American workers work 8 to 16 hours a day, but only produce real value that is equivalent to maybe one hour. A lot of that time is spent on "fluff." That's right. People screwing around on social media or messing around with email.

If you want to be serious about your career, your business, and all the other important stuff in your life, focus on work. This means focusing on the big objectives and putting in the necessary work to make those big objectives become a reality. Otherwise, you are going to be chasing your tail. You are going to run out of will power and energy because you spent those resources on things that ultimately don't matter all that much.

A good starting point would be to devote 30 minutes in the middle of your workday, and another 30 minutes to email and social media at the end of your workday. The bottom line here is that you only have a set amount of willpower to use daily. Use that willpower wisely.

Devote it to work. Devote it to things that would move your life forward. Restrict low impact activities that end up eating a lot of your time and willpower while returning very little value.

Sure, it's nice to get updates from your cousin that just came back from their trip to South America, and it would be nice to see email updates. But you need to restrict them to a few minutes every single day.

Otherwise, you are not going to develop the discipline you need to become a lean, mean, and efficient, goal-crushing machine.

Day 18: Practice

Practice day 17's techniques along with all the other previous techniques you learned from previous days.

These techniques flow into each other. They increase each other's value. Don't think that they are completely separated from each other. If you go through these days in the proper sequence, you would be able to turbocharge your self-discipline.

Remember, these days are all interconnected. You need to put in real effort into practicing the lessons of these days. Otherwise, you are not going to make much progress.

Practice:

- **Think Big**: Thinking about big objectives in your life

- **Set Specific Goals**: Figuring out specifically what you want to achieve those big objectives
- **Be Ruthless With Your Time**: Ruthless cut out "fluff" tasks and focus on the main items to achieve your goals – delegate everything else
- **See With Your Mind's Eye**: Visualize yourself having already accomplished your goals. Feel the excitement, passion, and confidence you would feel.
- **Rip Your Goals**: You want to have an emotional response to your goals. Writing and re-reading them is part of that. Ripping them and writing them again reinforces the desire, passion, and zeal you have toward your goals. You want to create as much emotion around them as possible – and of course, focus those emotions into action.
- **Get Comfortable Being Uncomfortable**: You need to get comfortable being uncomfortable. This will teach you to focus your energy and attention on your goals. Some examples are to start waking up earlier, take cold showers, resisting junk food, etc. The main point is to be conscious that you are doing this to develop focus and discipline; NOT to punish yourself. View it

as sharpening yourself, not wearing yourself down.

- **Create "Layers" of Focus**: Do the hard stuff and follow it up with easy stuff. The feeling of accomplishment and confidence will enhance your focus – not deplete it.

- **Sleep More, Eat Less**: Most of us eat too much and sleep too little. Focus on getting 7-8 hours of sleep and focusing on eating better. Be mindful when you eat, appreciate the flavors, chew slowly, enjoy your food. Eating more mindfully and sleeping more soundly will help sharpen your focus.

- **Restrict Social Media**: Yes, it's good to connect with friends, know what's going on in the world, and unwind. But use social media so that it does all of those things – not so it distracts you. Put in the work, then reward yourself by unwinding.

Day 19: The Power of Gratitude

"Focusing is about saying "No" – Steve Jobs

Write Down Three Things You Are Grateful For

On this day, you need to understand that your mindset governs how effective you are. That's right. Your external activities and the energy level you have are only products of internal activity.

What you choose to believe about yourself or any kind of situation has a direct role in how you behave. By simply changing how you think you would be able to change how you perform. Your physical activities may be easy to slice, dice, and measure, but they all flow from your decisions.

Your decisions, in turn, are products of your mindset. So, if you were to change your mindset, you will be able to achieve greater results. Here are two steps that would enable you to tap the power of your mental resources to become a more effective person all around:

Step 1. Quickly Write Down the Three Main Things You Are Grateful For Today

Keep in mind that these are things that are based on facts. You are not just intellectually listing stuff that you think you should be grateful for. You are not just listing down things that people tell you, you should be grateful for.

You should focus on realities, actions, and people, who truly provided something positive to you. These are people who made an impact in your life. These are things that really happened. It can be a small thing. Even small things can have a positive impact. Focus on facts, not just intellectual stuff. Don't focus on obligations. Focus on things that really mean something.

This way, you would focus on something real instead of simple vague feelings of gratitude. Such feelings can only go so far. If you want to really unleash your power of focus and pull a lot of energy from your emotional side, you need to focus on facts and things that really exist.

Step 2. Focus on Why You're Grateful for These Three Things

Write down three things that you are grateful for and zero in on why you are grateful for them. What is it about them that you feel so positive about? What is it about them that has such a tremendous impact on your life?

It's crucial to not just zero-in on a feeling, it's also crucial to get a logical and rational understanding. If you have both these areas covered: reasons and emotions, then things become more real to you. This is why I suggest that you spend quite a bit of time going through this exercise.

This is not something that you should do out of obligation. This definitely is not a "connect the dots" type of exercise. Under no circumstances should you simply go through the motions. This is serious stuff because the sooner you tap into the deep reservoir of gratefulness, the sooner you will deflect and redirect your mind's natural tendency to focus on itself.

The reason why a lot of people tend to spin around in circles and manage not to achieve anything in their lives, is because they're too self-absorbed. The ego takes a lot of energy when it's not focused. The best way to get a sense of focus is to disregard the ego and become more other-centered.

Believe it or not, many of the big billionaires and successful people in the world became big, not because they are fixated on making as much money off other people as possible, no. They got to the highest levels of success because they truly want to solve other people's problems.

This selflessness enabled them to build successful businesses and organizations. As the old saying goes, when you help others get what they want, you ultimately get what you want. You may be aiming for a million dollars but that is not going to happen unless you first solve other people's problems.

The more you solve other people's problems, the more they are likely to solve your problems. Your problem is cash flow, their problems involve better food, cheaper laundry, better dry cleaning, and so on and so forth. Do you see how this works? By focusing your mind to sidestep your ego, you go a long way in orienting your focus where it needs to go.

Day 20: Practice

Practice day 19's technique along with all other previous techniques.

Make sure that you spend enough time and effort rehearsing those previous techniques as well as Day 19's technique.

Keep in mind that these all flow into each other. The more you master one technique, the more you improve your other techniques. You can't just go through the motions. You have to go through the whole list.

Practice:

- **Think Big**: Thinking about big objectives in your life

- **Set Specific Goals**: Figuring out specifically what you want to achieve those big objectives
- **Be Ruthless With Your Time**: Ruthless cut out "fluff" tasks and focus on the main items to achieve your goals – delegate everything else
- **See With Your Mind's Eye**: Visualize yourself having already accomplished your goals. Feel the excitement, passion, and confidence you would feel.
- **Rip Your Goals**: You want to have an emotional response to your goals. Writing and re-reading them is part of that. Ripping them and writing them again reinforces the desire, passion, and zeal you have toward your goals. You want to create as much emotion around them as possible – and of course focus those emotions into action.
- **Get Comfortable Being Uncomfortable**: You need to get comfortable being uncomfortable. This will teach you to focus your energy and attention on your goals. Some examples are to start waking up earlier, take cold showers, resisting junk food, etc. The main point is to be conscious that you are doing this to develop focus and discipline; NOT to punish yourself. View it

as sharpening yourself, not wearing yourself down.

- **Create "Layers" of Focus**: Do the hard stuff and follow it up with easy stuff. The feeling of accomplishment and confidence will enhance your focus – not deplete it.

- **Sleep More, Eat Less**: Most of us eat too much and sleep too little. Focus on getting 7-8 hours of sleep and focusing on eating better. Be mindful when you eat, appreciate the flavors, chew slowly, enjoy your food. Eating more mindfully and sleeping more soundly will help sharpen your focus.

- **Restrict Social Media**: Yes, it's good to connect with friends, know what's going on in the world, and unwind. But use social media so that it does all of those things – not so it distracts you. Put in the work, then reward yourself by unwinding.

- **Be Grateful**: Being grateful allows you to focus on others, which opens them up to helping you. It also helps you be more creative, happy, and optimistic. It fosters good relationships and helps you maintain your focus.

Day 21: "Zen" Your Workspace

"If you chase two rabbits, both will escape"
–Unknown

Clear up your work and workout spaces
If you have a tough time working, whether at home or at an office, your problem might be due to simple clutter. That's right. When you see all sorts of mess around you, or your workspace is overly-complicated your willpower dissolves.

You have to remember that your focus needs to be amplified through simplification. You do this by removing as many distractions as possible. While this is not always doable, simplifying your workspace as much as possible can go a long way in fine tuning your focus.

Believe it or not, when you see all sorts of clutter, your focus can "leak." You may end up playing around with stuff that's leftover. You might end up messing around with some sort of gadget that you left lying around.

Since you only have so much focus on any given day, do yourself a big favor, by simplifying your workspace so you can focus your energies on the matter at hand. Once you've knocked out the big things, then you should allow yourself some leisure time.

The same approach applies to working out. If you are having a tough time hitting the gym on a consistent basis, it may be because the gym has so many different programs, machines, or other things going on.

Maybe the solution is to just go with a very simplified or stripped down gym. You might even buy equipment to set up your own ultra-simple home gym. You need to do whatever you need to do, to make sure that you have focus when you need it.

You should also be able to focus all your energies where they need to go. It's very hard to do this when you have so much clutter and distractions around you.

Day 22: Practice

Practice day 21's technique along with all previous techniques.

I hope you noticed that these techniques often alternate between mental things that you need to do, emotional management, and physical things. This is not random. They are in a certain sequence because they build on each other.

Make sure you not only implement these previous techniques and review them continuously, but you need to do them in the right order. You need to follow the order of these techniques so you can maximize their effects.

Practice:

- **Think Big**: Thinking about big objectives in your life
- **Set Specific Goals**: Figuring out specifically what you want to achieve those big objectives

- **Be Ruthless With Your Time**: Ruthless cut out "fluff" tasks and focus on the main items to achieve your goals – delegate everything else

- **See With Your Mind's Eye**: Visualize yourself having already accomplished your goals. Feel the excitement, passion, and confidence you would feel.

- **Rip Your Goals**: You want to have an emotional response to your goals. Writing and re-reading them is part of that. Ripping them and writing them again reinforces the desire, passion, and zeal you have toward your goals. You want to create as much emotion around them as possible – and of course focus those emotions into action.

- **Get Comfortable Being Uncomfortable**: You need to get comfortable being uncomfortable. This will teach you to focus your energy and attention on your goals. Some examples are to start waking up earlier, take cold showers, resisting junk food, etc. The main point is to be conscious that you are doing this to develop focus and discipline; NOT to punish yourself. View it as sharpening yourself, not wearing yourself down.

- **Create "Layers" of Focus**: Do the hard stuff and follow it up with easy stuff. The feeling of accomplishment and confidence will enhance your focus – not deplete it.

- **Sleep More, Eat Less**: Most of us eat too much and sleep too little. Focus on getting 7-8 hours of sleep and focusing on eating better. Be mindful when you eat, appreciate the flavors, chew slowly, enjoy your food. Eating more mindfully and sleeping more soundly will help sharpen your focus.

- **Restrict Social Media**: Yes, it's good to connect with friends, know what's going on in the world, and unwind. But use social media so that it does all of those things – not so it distracts you. Put in the work, then reward yourself by unwinding.

- **Be Grateful**: Being grateful allows you to focus on others, which opens them up to helping you. It also helps you be more creative, happy, and optimistic. It fosters good relationships and helps you maintain your focus.

- **Clear Up Clutter**: Nothing zaps focus like clutter and disorganization. Clear up your desk, your car, your room so that you feel calm, peaceful, and serene. This will help you feel focused and powerful.

Day 23: How to Instantly Change Your Mood

"Whenever you want to achieve something…
concentrate and make sure you know exactly
what it is you want"
–Paul Coelho

Put a pencil in your mouth and force yourself to smile. Did you know that even if you don't feel like smiling, looking like you're smiling can help you become more focused? Why? When your mood is elevated, you have more energy to focus. Your emotional state and your ability to focus and expand your willpower go hand in hand.

They are not mutually exclusive. They are definitely not separated from each other.

Best of all, when you choose to smile, you end up creating an upward spiral of energy. This is called a positive feedback loop.

When you make the first move, by forcing yourself to smile, other people, eventually, will bounce off those positive vibes back to you. When you smile at people and they smile back at you, you can't help but feel good, and this enables you to focus more and smile more.

Your smile then triggers another round of positivity from people around you and this can produce an ever-increasing spiral of positivity, energy, and a sense of possibility. Believe me, when it comes to personal focus, you need every little bit of help that you can get. There's just so many challenges and difficulties facing us in our daily tasks that it's very easy to run out of energy. This can happen very quickly as well.

By resolving to smile every day, you give yourself the gift of a boundless source of positivity and it doesn't cost you anything. Even if people don't smile back at you, you need to maintain that smile until you interact with somebody who can reciprocate.

Follow the steps below:

Step 1. Put a pencil in your mouth and bite it. Force yourself to smile.

Step 2. Take out the pencil and smile at people around you.

Step 3. If they smile back, broaden your smile. Allow yourself to savor the fact that you are able to get a positive reaction from them. Even if they don't smile back at you, keep smiling because eventually, you will get in front of somebody who will return your positivity.

Step 4. Rinse and repeat this process for ever increasing levels of emotional energy and focus.

Day 24: Practice

Practice day 23's technique along with other techniques learned from previous days.

Practice:

- **Think Big**: Thinking about big objectives in your life
- **Set Specific Goals**: Figuring out specifically what you want to achieve those big objectives
- **Be Ruthless With Your Time**: Ruthless cut out "fluff" tasks and focus on the main items to achieve your goals – delegate everything else
- **See With Your Mind's Eye**: Visualize yourself having already accomplished your goals. Feel the excitement, passion, and confidence you would feel.
- **Rip Your Goals**: You want to have an emotional response to your goals. Writing

and re-reading them is part of that. Ripping them and writing them again reinforces the desire, passion, and zeal you have toward your goals. You want to create as much emotion around them as possible – and of course focus those emotions into action.

- **Get Comfortable Being Uncomfortable**: You need to get comfortable being uncomfortable. This will teach you to focus your energy and attention on your goals. Some examples are to start waking up earlier, take cold showers, resisting junk food, etc. The main point is to be conscious that you are doing this to develop focus and discipline; NOT to punish yourself. View it as sharpening yourself, not wearing yourself down.

- **Create "Layers" of Focus**: Do the hard stuff and follow it up with easy stuff. The feeling of accomplishment and confidence will enhance your focus – not deplete it.

- **Sleep More, Eat Less**: Most of us eat too much and sleep too little. Focus on getting 7-8 hours of sleep and focusing on eating better. Be mindful when you eat, appreciate the flavors, chew slowly, enjoy your food. Eating more mindfully and sleeping more soundly will help sharpen your focus.

- **Restrict Social Media**: Yes, it's good to connect with friends, know what's going on in the world, and unwind. But use social media so that it does all of those things — not so it distracts you. Put in the work, then reward yourself by unwinding.

- **Be Grateful**: Being grateful allows you to focus on others, which opens them up to helping you. It also helps you be more creative, happy, and optimistic. It fosters good relationships and helps you maintain your focus.

- **Clear Up Clutter**: Nothing zaps focus like clutter and disorganization. Clear up your desk, your car, your room so that you feel calm, peaceful, and serene. This will help you feel focused and powerful.

- **Instantly Change Your Mood**: Want to feel happy, productive, confident, and well-liked? Smile at other people. Notice how much better you feel. Now use those positive feelings to get focused and work on what's important.

Day 25: Make it a Game

"To be everywhere is to be nowhere"
–Seneca

Set up daily games for your tasks
People are creatures of incentives. We tend to do what we do and act the way we act, because of some sort of reward. Let's put it this way; if you were punished quickly for doing an activity, chances are, you're not going to continue doing that.

For example, a kid that is learning to pick his or her nose is told by his or her parents that it's a bad habit and people might react negatively. The kid disregards his or her mom and continues to pick his or her nose. Eventually, some people look at the kid and laugh and this is enough for the kid to stop. They learned in a very simple yet effective way, that what they're doing is not rewarded. There is a disincentive to that kind of behavior.

The reverse also works. When you, for example, like to speak in class and you practice your public speaking skills so you are very clear, forceful, and effective, you probably will get a lot of applause. The more applause you get, the more motivated you are in finding public speaking opportunities. You end up fine tuning and honing your skills.

Incentives work. Do yourself a favor, and set up a daily ritual so you benefit from incentives.

Here is how you do it:

Step 1: Pick a reward for completing your daily to-do list. This reward doesn't have to be anything big. It doesn't have to cost a lot of money.

Step 2: Work on your to-do list until you reach the end.

Step 3: Enjoy your reward. This is crucial. You have to truly enjoy it. It means you have to emotionally soak it up. It has to be clear to you that what you are doing is enjoying your reward. You can't just go through the motions. You can't just zip through the reward, otherwise it won't feel like you are compensating yourself.

Step 4: Once you earn your reward five days in a row, add another item to your daily to-do list. This is crucial. Your ability to focus only grows if you challenge it. It's like a muscle. It's not going to grow if you're not going to put pressure on it.

The best way to grow your personal focus is to add more difficult things to your daily to-do list. Keep in mind that the reward that you choose for this technique must have two qualities. First, it must not cost much money.

There's no point in rewarding yourself with very expensive gifts. You don't want to drive yourself to the poor house. Second, the reward must not add pounds. In other words, it must not be fattening. The key here is to incentivize yourself and not blow yourself up as far as your weight is concerned.

Incentivize yourself to complete your to-do list and increase your focus. This would enable you to get a lot more things done within the space of eight hours.

Day 26: Practice

Practice day 25's techniques along with all other previous techniques.

Don't go through the motions. Do yourself a big favor and list them out and make sure that you practice all of them. Even if you were to do them very quickly, make sure that you actually do them and you pay attention to the quality of your experience. Don't leave anything out. Don't skip any details.

Practice:

- **Think Big**: Thinking about big objectives in your life
- **Set Specific Goals**: Figuring out specifically what you want to achieve those big objectives
- **Be Ruthless With Your Time**: Ruthless cut out "fluff" tasks and focus on the main items to achieve your goals – delegate everything else

- **See With Your Mind's Eye**: Visualize yourself having already accomplished your goals. Feel the excitement, passion, and confidence you would feel.

- **Rip Your Goals**: You want to have an emotional response to your goals. Writing and re-reading them is part of that. Ripping them and writing them again reinforces the desire, passion, and zeal you have toward your goals. You want to create as much emotion around them as possible – and of course focus those emotions into action.

- **Get Comfortable Being Uncomfortable**: You need to get comfortable being uncomfortable. This will teach you to focus your energy and attention on your goals. Some examples are to start waking up earlier, take cold showers, resisting junk food, etc. The main point is to be conscious that you are doing this to develop focus and discipline; NOT to punish yourself. View it as sharpening yourself, not wearing yourself down.

- **Create "Layers" of Focus**: Do the hard stuff and follow it up with easy stuff. The feeling of accomplishment and confidence will enhance your focus – not deplete it.

- **Sleep More, Eat Less**: Most of us eat too much and sleep too little. Focus on getting 7-8 hours of sleep and focusing on eating better. Be mindful when you eat, appreciate the flavors, chew slowly, enjoy your food. Eating more mindfully and sleeping more soundly will help sharpen your focus.

- **Restrict Social Media**: Yes, it's good to connect with friends, know what's going on in the world, and unwind. But use social media so that it does all of those things — not so it distracts you. Put in the work, then reward yourself by unwinding.

- **Be Grateful**: Being grateful allows you to focus on others, which opens them up to helping you. It also helps you be more creative, happy, and optimistic. It fosters good relationships and helps you maintain your focus.

- **Clear Up Clutter**: Nothing zaps focus like clutter and disorganization. Clear up your desk, your car, your room so that you feel calm, peaceful, and serene. This will help you feel focused and powerful.

- **Instantly Change Your Mood**: Want to feel happy, productive, confident, and well-liked? Smile at other people. Notice how much better you feel. Now use those positive feelings to get focused and work on what's important.

- **Reward Yourself**: Make a game out of completing your daily tasks. Humans are motivated by incentives, so make sure that you set up a reward for accomplishing your tasks. This will help you maintain your focus.

Day 27: Instantly Get Others to Help You

"A clear and focused mind will last a lifetime"
–Russell Simmons

Compliment at Least Five People Today
As I have mentioned previously, your ego can get in the way of focus. You only have so much focus on any given day. Unfortunately, if you waste that energy on yourself, you are less able to direct it to where it needs to go.

While confidence is a good thing, you should only be confident because of your skills. It is hard to start with confidence first and then build skills later. It usually doesn't work that way.

It would be better for you to focus on building up your willpower. Knock out some of the hard stuff that you need to take care of, and allow yourself to feel good so you can build your confidence on a solid bedrock of achievement and skill development.

To make this happen, you need to redirect your ego away from yourself. One of the best ways to do this is actually quite simple: compliment or praise other people. Here is how you do it.

Step 1. Find five people to praise.

Step 2. Give sincere praise.

By sincere praise, I'm talking about praising them for things that actually exist.
You're not idealizing them. You're not talking about them in theoretical terms (ie., you talk about stuff they can POTENTIALLY DO or BECOME), you are talking about stuff that they actually do, or traits that they actually possess in real life.

You should be able to come up with examples. For example, I truly appreciate your generosity. That discount ticket you gave me came in really handy.

It seems that you are the type of person who doesn't hesitate to help out his friends whenever they need anything. I'm so glad that you are my friend.

This is sincere because you zeroed in on a particular detail that is provable. It's not like you are just telling somebody, you're a great person because you make me feel great. That doesn't move the ball forward because it's too subjective.

If you're like most typical people, you would feel good about somebody one day, and then the next day, you would get irritated at them. It's much better to focus on things that are concrete and provable.

Step 3. Allow yourself to feel good that you have praised others.

This is the secret. While most of us can get around to sharing kind words to others, a lot of us feel so self-absorbed that we don't really feel the impact of that compliment. Allow yourself to feel good that you have praised others. This enables you to take your focus off your ego.

By taking your ego spotlight off yourself, your focus becomes others-directed. You open yourself up to getting more motivated by how much you help and benefit others. As I have mentioned previously, this is a big deal. The more you help others get what they want, the more likely it would be for them to help you get what you want.

You may be looking to buy a big house on the right side of town. You may be looking to drive a Ferrari or a Lamborghini, but that's the stuff that you want. It's going to be very hard for you to achieve those goals if you focus solely on benefiting yourself. People aren't just going to volunteer hundreds of thousands of dollars so you can drive a Ferrari.

Life doesn't work that way.

Instead, people have problems that need solutions. By focusing on how you can benefit them, and helping them achieve what they want, they can then help you get what you want by paying you. Do you see how this works? By being more "others-directed" you can achieve greater things with the same amount of focus.

There is also a second reason why you should compliment others. In addition to helping you establish a better relationship with your ego, making a habit of complimenting others deepens your ability to connect with others.

You are able to step into others' shoes, give them proper appreciation and acknowledgment and this ability to connect then can become second nature to you. You start seeking it out. It doesn't remain a skill that is only handy because it benefits you at some level or other. By being more others-centered, you can go quite far in life.

Day 28: Practice

Practice day 27's technique along with all other techniques. Learn from previous days.

Practice:

- **Think Big**: Thinking about big objectives in your life
- **Set Specific Goals**: Figuring out specifically what you want to achieve those big objectives
- **Be Ruthless With Your Time**: Ruthless cut out "fluff" tasks and focus on the main items to achieve your goals – delegate everything else
- **See With Your Mind's Eye**: Visualize yourself having already accomplished your goals. Feel the excitement, passion, and confidence you would feel.
- **Rip Your Goals**: You want to have an emotional response to your goals. Writing

and re-reading them is part of that. Ripping them and writing them again reinforces the desire, passion, and zeal you have toward your goals. You want to create as much emotion around them as possible – and of course, focus those emotions into action.

- **Get Comfortable Being Uncomfortable**: You need to get comfortable being uncomfortable. This will teach you to focus your energy and attention on your goals. Some examples are to start waking up earlier, take cold showers, resisting junk food, etc. The main point is to be conscious that you are doing this to develop focus and discipline; NOT to punish yourself. View it as sharpening yourself, not wearing yourself down.

- **Create "Layers" of Focus**: Do the hard stuff and follow it up with easy stuff. The feeling of accomplishment and confidence will enhance your focus – not deplete it.

- **Sleep More, Eat Less**: Most of us eat too much and sleep too little. Focus on getting 7-8 hours of sleep and focusing on eating better. Be mindful when you eat, appreciate the flavors, chew slowly, enjoy your food. Eating more mindfully and sleeping more soundly will help sharpen your focus.

- **Restrict Social Media**: Yes, it's good to connect with friends, know what's going on in the world, and unwind. But use social media so that it does all of those things — not so it distracts you. Put in the work, then reward yourself by unwinding.

- **Be Grateful**: Being grateful allows you to focus on others, which opens them up to helping you. It also helps you be more creative, happy, and optimistic. It fosters good relationships and helps you maintain your focus.

- **Clear Up Clutter**: Nothing zaps focus like clutter and disorganization. Clear up your desk, your car, your room so that you feel calm, peaceful, and serene. This will help you feel focused and powerful.

- **Instantly Change Your Mood**: Want to feel happy, productive, confident, and well-liked? Smile at other people. Notice how much better you feel. Now use those positive feelings to get focused and work on what's important.

- **Reward Yourself**: Make a game out of completing your daily tasks. Humans are motivated by incentives, so make sure that you set up a reward for accomplishing your tasks. This will help you maintain your focus.

- **Complement and Help Others**: Complimenting others is a way to take the focus off of yourself and onto others. This allows you to connect with them sincerely and honestly. The by-product is that they will want to help you achieve your goals, share their resources, and give you opportunities you may have never had. Also, notice how good it makes you feel. Use those good feelings to maintain focus toward your goals.

Day 29: How to Use Sex to Your Advantage

"The successful man is the average man, focused"
–Unknown

Restrict and Refocus Your Sexual Energy

This advice is extremely important because most human beings are driven by a strong sex drive. Unfortunately, without proper management, this drive can end up using up a lot of your focus. A lot of the personal energy that you have devoted to being more successful in life would end up being wasted on untargeted sexual energy.

I divided the advice below into two parts. One part is for single people, and the other part is for married individuals. Still, regardless of whether you are single or married, you need to pay attention to this day's technique because it can go a long way in helping you channel your personal resources so they can go to where you need them to go and you end up walking away with more achievements and victories in your life.

Single People

Step 1. Avoid porn

Seriously. Pornography, especially Internet porn, soaks up a lot of energy. It also soaks up a lot of your thinking time. Worst of all, it can easily become a habit. That's right. There is such a thing as porn addiction and just like nicotine addiction, or alcoholism, it can suck up tremendous focus.

Why? When you're thinking about your addiction, you're not focused on where you need to be. You're not emotionally engaged to such an extent that you would find the energy, power, and direction you need to crush your goals in the here and now.

Step 2. Re-focus that energy into your workouts or work

Now that you have refocused your energy on your romantic partners, it doesn't take much more effort to then refocus some more of that energy to your gym workouts or the stuff you do at work.

Step 3. Create an upward spiral

This requires a little bit of doing. But the sooner you get this working, the more powerful you will become. Create an upward spiral where the more you re-focus, the more you get things done. The more you get things done, the better you feel about yourself and this gives you the tremendous drive to refocus some more.

At the end of this process, you would have totally diverted what would otherwise be a confusing and frustrating waste of sexual energy and convert that into goal-crushing ability.

Married People

Step 1. Stop desiring other members of the opposite sex except your spouse

If you are a typical married person, you probably still look at members of the opposite sex. Now it's perfectly okay to look at good looking women and men, but you have to look at them based on their agenda.

In other words, stop looking at them as objects that have something to do with benefiting you. That's the big difference between looking at people in a sexual way and looking at them in a way that they deserve.

Good looking people should be acknowledged but you should not desire them because of how they benefit you. Look at them as people with their own unique needs or agendas and reasons. Now, this is probably going to take quite a bit of work because we have been programmed since we were young to look at others as objects or means to an end.

However, the better you get at this, the more effective this technique would be. You no longer look at people as gateways to some sort of sexual fulfillment or advantage. Instead, you look at them as people that are worthy of empathizing with. They have their own problems, agendas, and their own distinct take on the world.

If you are able to do this, you kill two birds with one stone. First, you stop wasting precious sexual energy and channel it to where it needs to go. Second, you are able to deepen your ability to connect with people and this can pay off tremendously in other areas of your life.

You connect with people not because they can do something for you, but you connect with them because they themselves have intrinsic value.

Step 2. Focus on pleasing your partner emotionally

Now that you have refocused a lot of your previously misdirected sexual energy, you can use this focus to get the drive you need to please your partner more. Do favors for them. Spend time with them. Give them gifts. Do what you need to do to make them feel loved.

Different people have different "love languages." By this time, you already know what your spouse's love language is.

Do more of that. Get the focus you need to do that and help them feel loved.

Step 3. Focus on pleasing your partner physically

Sex is still part of the equation. Improve your sexual performance not for your pleasure, but to increase the pleasure of your partner. This is crucial because you become others-directed.

The focus of sex is no longer to get pleasure out of somebody, but to give that person pleasure. This truly changes your perspective and enables you to be more effective when it comes to providing services at work, tackling problems, or simply reaching out to people and trying to understand them on a deeper human level. A little bit of selflessness goes a long way.

Day 30: Practice

Practice day 29's techniques along with all other techniques learned from previous days.

Practice:

- **Think Big**: Thinking about big objectives in your life
- **Set Specific Goals**: Figuring out specifically what you want to achieve those big objectives
- **Be Ruthless With Your Time**: Ruthless cut out "fluff" tasks and focus on the main items to achieve your goals – delegate everything else
- **See With Your Mind's Eye**: Visualize yourself having already accomplished your goals. Feel the excitement, passion, and confidence you would feel.

- **Rip Your Goals**: You want to have an emotional response to your goals. Writing and re-reading them is part of that. Ripping them and writing them again reinforces the desire, passion, and zeal you have toward your goals. You want to create as much emotion around them as possible – and of course focus those emotions into action.

- **Get Comfortable Being Uncomfortable**: You need to get comfortable being uncomfortable. This will teach you to focus your energy and attention on your goals. Some examples are to start waking up earlier, take cold showers, resisting junk food, etc. The main point is to be conscious that you are doing this to develop focus and discipline; NOT to punish yourself. View it as sharpening yourself, not wearing yourself down.

- **Create "Layers" of Focus**: Do the hard stuff and follow it up with easy stuff. The feeling of accomplishment and confidence will enhance your focus – not deplete it.

- **Sleep More, Eat Less**: Most of us eat too much and sleep too little. Focus on getting 7-8 hours of sleep and focusing on eating better. Be mindful when you eat, appreciate the flavors, chew slowly, enjoy your food.

Eating more mindfully and sleeping more soundly will help sharpen your focus.

- **Restrict Social Media**: Yes, it's good to connect with friends, know what's going on in the world, and unwind. But use social media so that it does all of those things – not so it distracts you. Put in the work, then reward yourself by unwinding.

- **Be Grateful**: Being grateful allows you to focus on others, which opens them up to helping you. It also helps you be more creative, happy, and optimistic. It fosters good relationships and helps you maintain your focus.

- **Clear Up Clutter**: Nothing zaps focus like clutter and disorganization. Clear up your desk, your car, your room so that you feel calm, peaceful, and serene. This will help you feel focused and powerful.

- **Instantly Change Your Mood**: Want to feel happy, productive, confident, and well-liked? Smile at other people. Notice how much better you feel. Now use those positive feelings to get focused and work on what's important.

- **Reward Yourself**: Make a game out of completing your daily tasks. Humans are motivated by incentives, so make sure that you set up a reward for accomplishing your tasks. This will help you maintain your focus.

- **Complement and Help Others**: Complimenting others is a way to take the focus off of yourself and onto others. This allows you to connect with them sincerely and honestly. The by-product is that they will want to help you achieve your goals, share their resources, and give you opportunities you may have never had. Also, notice how good it makes you feel. Use those good feelings to maintain focus toward your goals.

- **The Sex Advantage**: Use your sexual instincts to learn discipline and self-control. If you're married, use it to build love, gratitude, appreciation, and happiness. These positive feelings will further help you with staying focused on your goals.

Message Me

This book reveals simple exercises to **_unleash_** your potential, **_defeat_** procrastination, and **_unlock_** your productivity.

This book is just the beginning.

Reach out to connect.

And take action.

Do you want help?

Do you want to go deeper?

Do you want to ask questions?

Do you want to see how to apply this in real life?

If this book sparks something in you, don't let it fade.

Connect with me here: linktr.ee/razaimam

🖩 Book a 1:1 call

📞 Speak with me directly

📩 Join my private email list

🎁 Claim your free bonuses

🎥 See behind-the-scenes strategies

📇 DM me on LinkedIn, X, or Instagram

Reach out and take action.

All in one place: linktr.ee/razaimam

www.AuthorPreneurElite.com

Please Leave a Review – It Means a Lot

I hope you enjoyed this book. If you did, please leave me a review. It will only take 30 seconds and it would mean a LOT to me as an author.

We live and die by reviews:

- They help us know how our readers feel about our work
- They give us the motivation to keep writing
- They help others learn about our books

So please leave a review now.
Thanks in advance!